REFLECTIONS

A COLLECTION OF POEMS

SOMNATH BARUI

To Gitarani Barui and Late Narayan Ch. Barui, my parents whose
upbringing has nourished my inner self. To Pallabi, my mistress
who always encourages...

Contents

Contents

Preface

These poems are composed with no particular method in mind. Readers may find for themselves that most poems don't follow any rhythmic pattern or metrical schemes also. I have wilfully avoided that to make the readers experience variety of themes and styles. I have experienced a common procedure while penning these: spontaneous expression. A flash of a line has, more often than not, been felt to be the starting point of most poems. Some poems are there, like the poem *Once While Crossing the Padma*, that have been written twice, and in case of the instance quoted, the second attempt has been retained. Poems, I feel, are nothing but the natural niggle that the mind receives from inwards, and once the inward urge is heard, poems begin to well up in profusion. But in almost all poems, I have attempted to display an admixture of thoughts and inspired feelings, that reveals something idealistic and beautiful and bestows greater charm and meaning on human life.

1. The Dead Bird

O, catch the aura!
The aura of a moan
For a bird forlorn—
A small hapless bird
Has fallen softly apart;
It's crying for a requiem.
Humans are speeding by
None is 'till nearing nigh.
Its lifeless body lies
Breaking all the ties
With its dear abode, the earth,
Its kith and kin, its bowery hearth
Of trees, shrubs and all—
How can it endure such mortal fall?
Compassion old is dying so soon
From human heart, a glorious boon--
Lo! How fast their vehicles are flying
Past the bird, past all its crying…
How the fleeting beauty does pass!
Catch the aura, o you ignorant mass!
Surround the beauty, hold it high,
Behold it well to bewail and sigh--
Never in life has it striven for a thing

As low as humans oft do incur in--
It deserves a goodbye, warm and solemn.
Lo! How on the left and right
Smile the corns green and bright,
The sun above is mild and slow
Wind has its mercurial blow—
It's a day not worth for a beauty to die;
Sigh, o humans! Come and only sigh.
The trees nearby are at their bloom,
Removing the winter's normal gloom—
The grass-flowers do peep and see
The farmers at their wonted glee,
But none can call their helpful hand
To attend any aviary death-song grand.
However far the eyes can reach
Same phenomena persist that only teach:
Every bit of event that happens here,
Whatever nature it, in itself, does bear —
Be it sad, jolly or a mixture of both—
Will continue the same with a life-growth
That none can break or breach at all
No rules dominate its build-up or fall.
For, time will come and time will go,
Ignoring such footprints of sorrow.

2. Realization

When my father died, someone asked,

'How do you feel now that your father's no more?'

I unmindfully said, 'The sun's being felt on my back a bit more.'

The inquisitor beamed a little and stopped her query.

Her smile hinted at my phrase perhaps being deep-meaning.

Later I mused inwardly and found, maybe it was.

My father who ran our family,

Kept no stone unturned to bring smiles on our faces.

His excessive careful endeavour beggars praise.

From sunrise till sundown he, as if, under a trance

Performed his hard-work with gasps and hungers;

His hard-work was our sense of relief, our hope.

He was an umbrella spreading shades

Over us like a canopy of sweet dreams—

Hardness of soil was then, to me, a faraway voice—

Indistinct, unheard, unfelt and happily forgotten.

When big trees cover the shrubs underneath,

They ensure protection of all sorts for them.

My father was a big tree protecting us, the shrubs

From the myriad afflictions of this feverish world.

His care seemed more invaluable, more real,

His hard-work now seems love, truer than love itself.

The sun when he was alive was the same as it was after—
Only difference was the shade was gone from over me.
'I've to try to make another shade,' I thought.

3. The Hind Story

The book I see in front has a story—
It's all so quietly forgotten all these days.
That day it was raining hard,
Possibly thundering also,
I don't remember.
The train was late unusually.
I remember the jostling crowd in the train.
Then the struggle with getting a seat in the bus—
When I reached College Street the weather calmed down;
I didn't go for a single book.
In fact I bought some, necessary for my PhD
But this book, a book of poetry criticism
Took hold of me—
I took no extra space with me—
The bag was full to the brim.
But I didn't back away.
The uncanny happened: I forgot to encase it.
It, paid and belonging to me, remained on the counter.
When I was in the taxi, worrying the driver up,
Telling him to let me get hold of the 6:30 evening train,
I subconsciously remembered my dear delight.
A sense of irritation was engulfing me,
I remembered all how I had lost it.

Then the reworking up my way to the shop,
Buying an extra bag to bag it safe,
Bearing with the shopkeeper's sarcastic stare,
Expending extra money amounting to half
Of the book's price, expending energy,
Patience and huge amount of time,
Keeping my family members in extra worry—
I have done a lot for this book,
I now vividly recall all of it.
It's not a big story or big achievement
Or desiring to glorify the self-immolation—
It's a nuance of a remembrance.
But this is really important for me
For, nuances are life.
Moreover, it has become 'my' book.

4. The Self-Centered

Happy are only they,
As the likes of Keats say,
Who are extremely selfish,
Or, to specify, more wolfish
For meeting their personal gains
And all; those who take no pains
To bother about the moral side
Of a thing and take long stride
To kill every human flower in man
By thorny means; they only plan
How to make money and be obtuse
And give a deaf ear to and confuse
The call of the soul. They know best
The meal, the pelf, the sleep and the rest—
Such a life is really the eighth wonder
For, mustn't we humans prick and ponder?

5. Hymn to a Mother

Each mother tells a fairy tale
Of imaginary feats and deeds
Unperceived by the common masses
Pains she holds in her bosom
The pains of household chores
The pains of diversified afflictions
Starting from bearing the burden
Of breasts to the begetting
And nurturing of children—
The pain multiplies along with
The increasing of the number
Of children she is often forced to bear—
Often…
She never complains, she accepts
With a peaceful resignation
With a calm that we scarce can think of—
Her myriad painful experiences are nothing but
An extension of our indifferent social codes—
All forbearance of hers is an altar
For her to be eternally worshipped;
She is an already beatified wonder.
She is the best saint humans can dream of.

6. A Simple Sermon

Life is a continuous wonder, a rare fuller mystery
On the huge void of the vast universe, piling only history
Of things and events, known or unknown,
And with utmost show of insouciance goes on and on.
Life on the void—can even the science-men expound?
There's no thread, but we're so infallibly bound.
Thus, most we may do of it all that's here
Is to show a 'human' spirit, and its wealth share.

7. The Greater Consciousness

Anthropologists say, the dinosaurs were hit
By a huge asteroid sixty-six million years ago.
The lives on earth were all shattered
To pieces, to mere dust. The dust of Adam
Not yet formed to a physique till then,
As they tell us, the anthropologists wise.
Poor creatures of the earth! Poor predecessors
Of ours! They scarcely could know anything—
They perished before they knew. The earth
Shook up so tremendously, the lives more so—
How uncertain lives are! How playable their dreams!
In this bountiful world and magnanimous universe,
Such ferocity inheres! Such, such ferocity!
The earth spins atop in the void, just like
A dangerous dance of a wanton toy,
Toying with human lives all the time around—
She is so full of loveliness, we simply awe.
Fierceness and beauty co-exist, but how?
Will our lives too, more beautiful and bountiful
Than any, perish like the dinosaurs at an instant?
Only the watch of Eternity knows best
What's in stock for our void-life.

8. The Couple

Science is but the man and literature his maid
One manages the reasoned affairs and the other instead
Looks after the decorating task of the soul
With a good heart and passion, for that's her goal.
The world at our hand is full with bleak things,
Full with afflictions, and hardness that brings
The choleric mould on our outer air, and just then
Science comes good with his myriad medicinal vein.
But for reasons numerous when our mind's sovereign sky
Is shrouded with a chiaroscuro and struggles to far fly
Or desires the sweet gentleness of a soft deft dealing
Literature and her daughter, Music, hustle to the healing.
Thus, as long as the couple, Science and Literature reign,
All live happy and free— the women and the men.

9. Deep into the Civilization

The certainty of civilization is a matter of
Long, long toil and overwhelming sacrifice
Of large number of innocent lives
Who obtained the hard-earned certitude
From the mystery-bedrabbled womb of nature
Have you ever thought how came the apples
That are so dearly valued today? How came the smile
Garnered from the fresh look of dear vegetables around?
Or how was the poison deciphered in certain earthly shrubs
And in trees and in certain roots
To give the salubrious certainty of the edibles?
Through sacrifice large and luminous!
Those of our ancestors sprawling across
Many generations and nations of the past
Killed themselves unwittingly while tasting the poison,
Unable in primitive ignorance to separate the nectar:
The lucky tasted the pomegranate, the unlucky mandragora.
Fear, suspicion and the superhuman mettle!
They searched for nature's boon all over,
Often succumbed to the bane mysteriously hidden.
Their life—a game of the musical chair—
Did either shine in or was darkened out—

And the suffering continued through the dark ages
Of plagues and epidemics down to the present time.
We are still going through unknown diseases, discoveries,
Inventions and renovations for the future generations.
All previous deaths are a pure sacrifice at the altar of humanity.
Between a father and a son, there's this history of fragrant sacrifices
Each father-bud has led to the son-flower for ages
Life's all about the search for our primal sources

10. Peace after Burning

The paralytic died today
Leaving all in relief behind
The old haggard kept dirtying the household
And emitting abrupt loud cries
Of pain now and then
Oh! He must have been a sinner!
Life was a hell all these days.
He has been cremated.
No more cries, yells, no disturbance
Peace is in burning after all
The one-time guardian of the house
At last ended his life as a perfect nuisance
Even more than a nuisance!
Especially to his family members
His old wife day and night cursed him
Oh! What sense of irritation was in her voice!
What a great declension!
What mysterious play of things unknown!
The neighbours also will now have
A happy sleep full of sweet dreams

11. Death's Absences

Death has no compensation—
When one dies, one misses Life's magnet
That holds every living organism together;
One misses the myriad dear sensations,
Moments outstanding and divine of love,
Of a certain deed of mercy and care,
Of a simple jolly gossip with dear ones,
Of some simple subtle relish of a loveliness
Derived from the blue sky sparsely overcast,
From the mild tossing heads of dancing shrubs—
Life can't be substituted by any wondrous means,
For, she's the most beautiful of wonders imaginable.
Life's the birth and nourishment of a curious feeling,
The philosophy, the search for epiphanies of existence,
The tantalising charm of a fairy in a dream—
Life's the eternal maid with all her chiaroscuro.
Death ends all of it in a flash—
The sensations sweet and sour, the feelings
Rare and fantastic are abruptly put to an end,
Like the switching off of a bulb at night-time—
Everything's dark and gone so soon.
Death is a darkness, an absence of all light
That Life sustains.

Whoever of us likes this gloom, this pit of all absence?
Death's the world's end, the last chapter of a story
With its magnificent appeal of many queries—
Death deprives a soul of the vibrating Life
Who enamours it each day with new potentials
And hopes that never, never wish to be extinct—

12. A Remembrance

When I heard my grand-mom was dead,
I was silenced for a while.
The lady was the rarest mould I have known:
Her smiling reception was a gift.
Why couldn't I return her the cost of the gift?
The inner beauty of the gift is with me for ever,
Her affections sweet and lovely are in my veins.
I forgot all this while she was alive—
The complex imbroglio of clouds shrouded me,
I didn't see beneath the skin of things.
I felt so helpless. I can't clone her beauty of presence anymore.
I had promised her I would visit her with a new set of tidings
That would bring her joy and me a satisfaction
But not to be, never to come to pass!
I couldn't keep my words;
I was busy with flesh and blood,
With happiness that engrossed me,
With forgetfulness that defiled me—
It is getting bitterer day by day.
She perhaps had searched for me,
Perhaps she had all the time hoped I'd come to her.
She died with a heart sore and vacant,
That can never be replenished—

Cruel life doesn't give one the second chance.
All my hopes of regaining her gloss of presence
Are a futility, that will run a lifetime.
O cruel remembrance! O knawing conscience!
I have created a vacuum somewhere
In the deep depth of my being

13. My Buying a Pair of Shoes

I went for buying a pair of medicated shoes
From a standard famous shoe showroom in Burdwan
I had travelled two and a half hours
My attire, shirt and pants, got shoddy and shabby naturally
Ours is a land of dust!
I asked the counterman: 'May I get a pair of shoes?'
Giving me a hard critical stare of doubt he said,
'Yes, the shoes are available but costly.'
He insinuated my inability of buying any,
Considering me as a have-not probably, not fit enough
To visit that costly showroom—
He was no owner, only a salesman sort.
I inwardly thought, 'This man is a typical case.'
I have often seen owners excelling themselves in decorum.
Later I came out of it after having a pair for each of us
My friend, when he heard the case from me, insinuated back,
'Next day we shall come wearing lungis.'
I laughed heartily and forgave the man.

14. The Unfathomable

What is that urge, that unknown potency
That snaps a life up from all leniency?
Lost lives are a source of grief, no doubt
But the self-killed ones are a question stout,
Pointing at the mystery of the world's origin
Out of nowhere into the spatial void divine.
Happy is the bird in her bower and secure
And lovely is the air prancing with a lure
Around the coiling shrubs near the hearth
Where the human child once had its birth—
The sky is in its darling beauteous hue,
The little moving buds leave no cue
For the excessive joy they bring forth,
It's all so serene and a wonder's worth—
It's all so serene and incites a life-zeal
In a human eternally who can only feel
The deft soft titivations of the deep desire
For a happy outing in this life-vale of pleasure—
Beauty here, beauty there, beauty everywhere
That thus beckons a human soul to take its care.
But the failing mind instead thinks of things bleak
And black and sour that awfully stick
Until...where does the power come from?

The power of negating learnt values all,
The power of sniffing away beauty's call—
The potential of invoking the final pain
Puzzles those left behind, the normal brain,
And is the primitive man's gamble of his life
Spent among the deadly beasts and in woeful strife—
But even as the rose that bears the thorns,
The beauty of life has its diverse chiaroscuro morns.
Who prioritizes the thorns? None but the one
Who has never seen the coming up of the dawn
From the utmost dark womb of nature's prime
That only tells: 'Whatever the hurdle, let it be,
For it'll vanish up in your rising majesty.'

15. An Alternative

Is there an alternative sane, sound and mild
To the world's religiosity ancient and wild?
Religion's a heart's child, born long time ago
To give men right route to remove fear or ego,
To let them believe that 'humanity' is the key
That helps unlock the burden of life's mystery
And keep the beacon of good work burning bright.
All's changed since power-mongers ascended
The self-made thrones, and mercilessly decapitated
The shining glory blossoming inside a Bruno or a Joan
That black deed of religiosity is still on, as we know,
And often is seen to wear civilization's mask and go
Unchecked and unshorn, for they've at last ingrained
Into our human mould and been, as if, ordained.
The world's history doesn't accolade the preachers
Of religion all, neither hold them good as teachers
Of humanity vast and vital for the world's sake
For, who wants the sacred altar held by the ferocious and the
fake?
Religious formulas have ever abided by the nine nooses
That have wreaked havoc on society's morale, that looses
Their bleak poison still on human endeavours all.
Divisions of caste and creed, high and low befall

Unto the most glorious race sustaining the beauty
And glamour of nature, turning it into a cosmic nicety
The alternative's a costly one, like whirling water's force
Taking time in a bucket for following the opposite course,
Must take the human toil, patience and huge turmoil
Before being moved onto its sovereign soil—
Let's hold festivals local, national or international
Deeming the degrees of contribution to causes social
Of humans mightier and more humane than the common block,
Whose lives became shrines of delight with overwhelming stock
Of wealth, near and dear to the human heart eternal
How could we have borne the indecencies all?
Let's celebrate a Sadi, or a Hafiz, or a Shakespeare, or a Copernicus—
With the days of their great deeds or their luminous birthdays in focus,
Let's celebrate, in the same vein, the glorious feats
Of a Rabindranath or a Marie Curie or an awful Keats
Or a Spinoza or a Descartes or a Derrida or a social reformer of note
Who worked for the society at large, not for a lone sect's selfish mote,
None from no religion's selfish, narrow-viewing den
Shall astoundingly venture forth to outright disdain
Such glorious celebration, nor can forestall its flight

Throughout the fragrant air to the ethereal height
No killing, no pollution for religion's sake
Would spoil human heart or a tragedy make—
All will stay here, with feet glued to the earth
Heroes will be celebrated to the utmost mirth
Amidst drums and sticks and garlands sweet,
Amidst remade songs, and cuisines meet—
The human heroes would neither be the prey
To the superstitious claim that 'they did betray
The spirit being encircled or possessed by God supreme,
For, who else but that power could perform to such extreme?'
Heroes will be heroes, bespeckled by a true praise,
A proper race of humans emerge, inured to apt phrase
All religious bigotry, all religiosity's age-old stain
May thus be washed away by such renovating rain

16. The Ridiculous

The ridiculous is the norm
Be ready to fit in
All your tradition of values you must bury
Under the debris of your unconforming mind
Look around today and try to recognise
The traces of the moral, human values
Taught to you so long ago in schools
Not an iota of them left
The desiccation of man's opportunistic recklessness
Has sucked up the morals to the dregs
What's a society or a system of politics
Bereft of a pristine fellow-feeling and love?
We live outwardly
The inner sanctity is long dead
So, don't hope for a rejuvenation
Hope for a conglomeration of anomalies
Patched up with a false decency
The great Jibanananda was right,
'Dawn dawns in the ever expansive dark.'
These are hard times, my people
Harder than what Dickens ever knew.

17. Democracy

Democracy is sung all day here
Through this or that 'little' incident
Always people get a political companion
In days of their woe—in times of flood,
Family feud or political extermination,
Or excommunication or mishap of any insignificance
This is an age of 'leaders' who never went to school
Or had an academic career in any sense
No Whitman will ever sing of a Lincoln again
That time is past.
'Leaders' with more criminal cases are a priority
For, only they can show red eyes to 'democracy' easily
And can obtain or embezzle votes for their concerned group.
They can help in the buying and selling of vote-products
With an insouciance hardly achievable by the truly cultured
They are always beside the woe-struck citizens or families
Who have been reportedly harmed by their own clan.
News channels are a continuous source of misrepresentation
Or highly intentional misrepresentation
For, they can also be bought nowadays.
Is there any worse cul-de-sac?
Any worse scenario of human degeneration?
History may cater different similar examples—

A Julius Caesar or a Wallace is there.
But how long?
Is it a heritage that we're taking forward?
The present seems to affirm exactly that.
The right to vote for all was hard-earned
But its loss is not so.
There's no sane brain that can rend the sky apart
And say: 'Stop the dirty game of politics
And come back with a propriety of democracy
We've always dreamed of.
Let no Martin Luther King Jr. be assassinated,
Nor a petty simple urchin be sacrificed
At the wrongly-conceived altar of election—
Let us value all life and move towards a saner, safer
democracy.'
There's none, for his voice will first be crushed.
We are living in a dehumanised world of anomalies.

18. O Whatsapp!

Is there a soul on earth who doesn't know
The omnipresent presence of Whatsapp?
The onus of newly arrived technology,
The greed of wasting more vacant time,
The freedom of mild lechery and self-treachery
And the endless rattle of chats and prattle
With elements principally vulgar and low—
We've already moved to the Whatsapp age—
The exchange of 'good morning', 'good night'
With big quotes from the stalwarts of literature,
Science, philosophy, sports and cinema;
The thousand ways of putting up cinematic 'Status'
On myriad matters as diverse as Thai thali to petty
sentiments—
This little app house keeps its charmed denizens
Glued to its magic world where Hamelin's miracle-man comes
With wondrously childish chats, photos and videos—
O the educated fertile world of the century!
The parents, the educating officials, the minor pupils,
The uneducated, the in-betweens and the low-wage
workers—
Whatsapp is the new usher of a world order, a leveller.
The greats of the world failed to do what it has achieved!

The dreamt-of act of 'levelling'—
None has any leisure except whatsapping.
The age of gardening, stamp-collecting, singing,
Reading, fishing, listening to music is past now—
Students remain online till two or three ante meridiem
And keep their fingers crossed for another Corona wave
To see them through the great hurdle of 'feared' exams
What more can Whatsapp perform?
We are like straw floating on the Whatsapp current so
securely!

19. Veronica

Be a Veronica, O Ukrainians!
You have a lot to fight still.
The surroundings have filled with bullet sounds—
Loud, piercing, distinct and terrible.
Sing your heart out with pianos
And cover the hell with music's tuneful heaven!
Sound shrouds sound, Veronica!
Only you have shown the war maniacs a way—
When the Russians are emptying their tank of bullets
Or readying for a fresh attack with bomb squads,
Your tune-flower has acted as an ironic dart
Seeking to uproot the thorn of ancient congealed hatred
From those stubborn inhumane hearts
That don't shiver before man-slaughter,
Nay, dream-slaughter of a far more significant note.
Afghanistan bans women's education,
Gunmen in the broad daylight kill
Thousands of innocent budding babies—
We've witnessed many more over the years.
Veronica, splash up your music
Into the ethereal sky and ring out loud!
Be the mild remonstrating voice of those hearts
Who have known best what actually they have lost—

If there's anything called 'love'
You've known it, Veronica, only you
Who have seen the truth amidst all nonsense:
'The old ways of sovereignty must go on.'
When in the dead of night, my lidless eyes
Pierce the looming darkness and reach
The doorstep of those war-beruffled Ukrainians
Or their soul mates from any age of history,
I empathise their day-to-day struggles
With sanitation and shelter, food and medications,
Their deathly waiting without end for the unknown
And visualise their vibrant pain and protest,
I can't recognize or claim that we've come
To this day through Enlightenments;
That we've come through the travails of two World Wars;
Veronica, sweet pianist, let's make a pact:
We won't sing humanism anymore;
We would rather wait on to see the bleak extent
To which the hands of self-mockery might reach.
We would call up no Mother Teresa or Florence Nightingale,
But with listless eagerness observe
The expanded swollen red eyes of a new Hitler
Gathering with his charismatic skills
The bones of all killed innocents—
We shall only see, and listen to you, wise Veronica
For, we are at world's end, and nothing matters.

20. The New Race

I once called a Bengali news channel
All of a sudden, out of a stubborn wish
To enquire their business policy
For, more often than not, news channels
Are consigning viewers to passive consumerism—
The time was the gigantic leisure of pandemic;
I was anxiously expecting the channel to telecast
News regarding the present number of Covid cases,
I was hoping for lesser cases obviously.
My mood was that of a desperate soul
With his back against the wall—
But it was the same picture again:
Two minutes of news encumbered with
Five precious patient minutes of commercial ads!
Commercialism is inevitable, no doubt,
Loss and profit go hand in hand everywhere
But is it sanity for a broadcasting channel,
Showing human misery, to show unabashed commercialism?
And that even at the time of
A sorest sore in human history?
I gave it a long thought before making the call,
I didn't find enough reason against the decision.
And I did the ineluctable.

The man on the other side heard my question
After the initial exchange of essentials:
'Is there any cause for so many ads
In the midst of a piece of news, and especially
When it's time of a fearsome pandemic?'
The man uninterruptedly heard all and just
In a sombre, commercial voice added, 'What, ads?'
And he quickly cut off the call without any decorum.
It was clear he understood my meaning
But he was helpless, I thought—
He was one of those commercialists, who trade
Out of a 'new' compulsiveness in this 'new' world
The trade of unscrupulous phoney social reformism—
His duty is to avoid all 'humane' thoughts,
To shirk off the dregs of all compassion
And be popular, be reliable and be the 'first'
To telecast any new 'food' for the consumers—
In the general board meetings his bosses moulded
His psyche, and taught him how to put on a façade
Of culture, humanity, care and dedication
With the pomp and show of new modes of presentation—
It was an epiphany for me, a darkening light
That gave only the glimpses of gloom around—
The accumulation of power, pelf and position,
The race for being 'first' in the competition
In the growing markets of broadcasting, health and
education—

Are the 'new' normalcies of this new-found world:
A world found with the utmost care
That no chance of publicity should sieve thro' the fingers.
This overwhelming race makes up the 'new' human race.

21. Distance

I have not bidden you adieu yet
And will never do so till my last breath
You are as secure in my memory and life
As a snail inside its time-proved shell
Your absence has tortured me physically
For I still can feel the fragrance of your proximity
Time's ineluctable demon, through its agent of misunderstanding,
Has erected a heavy semi-transparent giant-wall between us,
Depriving me of your perfumed presence
But please don't worry, my friendly philosopher-guide—
I have, all this while, got a spiritual wire invisible
That has kept me connected to you—
This wire is my wisdom supplier.
Whenever my disabled world-weary brain fades
And looks for some divine inspiration,
This invisible boon caters me with healing antidote,
Things and teachings eternal supplied to me
By your higher helping hand—
I harvest gold from your memory.
Your presence is reactivated and rejuvenated,
And I am again your pupil of yore.
As long as there is natural rain in this fevered world,

I will continue drenching the root of my reverence for you,
For my feeling is pure and natural.
Whenever I remember my father dear, I remember you.
You both can safely sit side by side on my mind's altar
As the equal shareholders in the little success
Life has bestowed me with.
The wire is getting firmer and stronger day by day
As your words and sermons are proving cumulatively vital
In my perceptions of reality of all sorts—
In this age when 'teaching' is multi-polluted,
In this age when teachers are bought and sold,
You seem to be a bright beacon spreading assurance:
'There's still hope for humanity, there's light.'
Let every raindrop of my revered prayer for you
Fall on both sides of the erected wall till
They flood out the sore visibility
And bring us closer to what we were.

22. Only You

I won't promise otherwise at all.
Like a time-honoured Romeo, I can't
Hoodwink all and visit you in the night
And utter prolix metaphors and hyperboles;
I can't, like an Antony, shirk all duties
And ignore the scruples of my fevered mind—
I can't fly to you like a modern hero
Flying countries for proximity wild—
No, I won't promise otherwise
But that I will keep the bud of our feeling
Intact, and water it and let it mature
Into a blossom-bearing tree;
I will crawl to you, my dear
In that I will stay aground and simple
I won't promise what evaporates
On the hard soil of testing time's ordeal
I will crawl to you and look all around
The society where we two belong,
The ground will make our feet hard
Along with the ordeal-burnt soul
To smooth out the rough edges of reality

23. Cooking

I like cooking a lot.
I don't say it as a euphemism although
My wife has in no way forced it
And doesn't enjoy me drudging along
In the punishment room called kitchen
I cook fairly well, they say
But in cooking I find a procedure—
Today I all of a sudden discovered it—
The procedure of pain reaching to success:
The recipe, if followed arduously to the end,
With the expected patience and skill and labour
Mixed with a self-belief, brings tasty success.
It is an art, of course—a neat job of beauty.
Cooking conforms to art and life-struggle,
Both of which involve a procedure of pain and pleasure.
What's more there to get from a mortal act?
Cooking in a way resembles me,
Looks like me in my struggle of a decent existence
In this indifferent world where each human pines
In the desert of humanity and none can hear—
An artist best knows the cost of his artefact.

24. The Social Code

Old Lila Samanta is a darling lady.
She can smile with all people with a good heart.
What else is there in the world more vital?
But the dear soul is unhappy.
A grave medical issue has intervened.
She can't digest food now.
Doctors have prescribed her soft diet.
Poor Lila grandma wails to her daughters-in-law:
'What do I eat? Only vegetables and rice.'
The daughters-in-law Sohini and Kavita are in a fix:
'How can we cook her oil-free veg curry', they demur,
'The doctors won't spare us if they know.'
Lila grandma has been taking veg meals
For over thirty years now—that's in itself
A feat that equals some great feats of the world—
After the demise of Gadadhar, her husband—
Indian women perform unsung miracles.
Initially it was tough to get on
Without her favourite dish, fish-curry.
But Hindu society's rules and inevitability interposed
And she decided to be another Gandhari—
To live a death-like life for saving Gadadhar's name—
Time is taking its toll on her now.

How dearly she wishes to grab non-veg dishes!
But for thirty years she has been smelling daily,
And daily ignoring the non-veg scents
For righteously observing her sacred promise.
Once for a while, she tried to hoodwink
And for some days took her dear dish secretively,
But since the advent of clever Kavita, youngest daughter in law
She shirked it all, fearing discovery
And the resultant infamy and humiliation.
Now as she hears the indistinct bell of her final call
She is getting irritable and stubborn:
The daughters in law must cook her oily food
Or she would fast, she has threatened.
She can't take it any longer.
The Suttee Rite burned girls and women alive
The Widow Rite's been killing women alive thro' odd restrictions
The so-called Brahmins, the best of the Hindus
Once devised such nooses for women,
Who have always sacrificed
For children and family everywhere.
Go through novels by Ashapurna Devi,
Many Lilas will knock at the door
Of your twenty first century conscience.
What is a life if devoid of the culinary choices,
Basic to any living organism.

Just take a deep breath and ponder
The best of the so-called race, Twice-born,
The creator of religious order in society;
Just think whether a life can be sacrificed
At the altar of some unconscientious rule thus!
A life is a life.
Its sorrows and joys are its own.
How can an obsolete code dictate its course?
Many Lilas have lost their lives ingloriously
Unnoticed, uncared, unthought for.
Many Lilas are suffering here and there still
In different corners of the Indian society.
Old Lila is having indigestion and vomiting
And the doctors opine she'll vomit if heedless
To the prescribed set of rules and meals.
Poor Lila says, 'God, come and take me.
What shall I do with this life?'

25. Daily Routine

Every day I've to follow a routine
In the bus I travel by to my office:
'O brother, can one smoke in the bus?'
This question of mine arouses humour
In some who know me as a protester.
The other passengers are a grand spectacle.
The smokers are normally shy and repetitive.
And sometimes they do grumble, and mumble too,
But I have kept the beacon of my itching duty burning.
Hoping to get new confederates I despair.
Nobody joins me in my just cause.
The smokers stare awkwardly and non-smokers blink.
What can a simple person like me do?
Nothing perhaps, and this is West Bengal—
Here the worthy hunger on the road
And the unworthy withdraw hefty salary per month.
Here the constitutionally powerful portfolios bet
And sell thousands of lives to 'chill penury'.
Smoking in the bus is a Lilliput issue
To call for the attention of...
No, no, it's a light battle
I'll knock the scruples of no office heavyweights
I'll go my own way and season

As a citizen of this once-famous Bengal
With many failures and frustrations

• 43 •

26. Once While Crossing the Padma

It's almost evening around the famed river
A misty stillness has unfolded everywhere
The lean strap of the river lies calm
Beneath a frozen winter sky, slightly tinged
By the chiaroscuro presence of the moon
The river Padma is all set
To welcome the guests
That daily gather over here.
But it's the moon, the aged youth
And the old overwhelming friend of the nostalgic
That has donned a new look today
How it beckons the helpless humans!
If anything in the world is true
It's your envious beauty, o Moon!
It's your unknown charm that leaves
The mind lonely and desolate all of a sudden—
Why on earth do we ply our selfish business?
Why do we eat and sleep ruthlessly
Without caring for this night's queen
Dangling in utter innocence from the mid-sky?
Is there anything truer and more soulful?
Do you know what the moon tells you,

You silly self-motivated money-monger,
You reckoner of opportunities low and vulgar?
Let me tell you.
All your life when you see such wetness,
Coupled with selfless love, in the sky goddess
Hold your breath and drink deep
Into the lunar spectacle for a while
And think where you are—
Floating midstream into the sky
With no foothold below your feet!
You've only one fantastic lifetime,
The life of a human!
You are lucky to escape the birth of an ant
That always dies in confused life!
You'll have goosebumps I guarantee.
You'll ever after ask for such evenings
When life's most valuable lesson surfaces
In that ethereal sky, the real teacher—
The greats of the world had this lesson from there
Before a human teacher taught them.
O Murshidabad, I thank you for this,
If not for anything else;
And I urge you to utter words of welcome
For this evening moon that is reflecting
Awfully in the Padma water with glee
And say, 'I hail you, Moon, I hail you
Into my life's newly built garden

Where I wish your eternal hand
In my daily feverish affairs.'
I'm no believer of God constructed
To swindle the uneducated masses—
I believe in the spiritual and the otherworldly
Brought into our busy conscious mind
By the likes of the sovereign Moon—
O Moon, be the guide to the troubled humanity!
They are tied all around by evanescent noose!
Free them and give them a life worth living.

27. The Obsession

The drunken, hazy thought of permanence!
Oh, what an unearthly joy in that!
That I came here and made it count!
Oh how refreshing and mightily soul-nourishing!
But permanence for how many days or years?
Apocalyptic scientists are on the prowl
For the assuring traces of life on other planets
If this world doesn't exist, then what?
Then, which people will remember me?
The transferred earth-companions?
Transferred for keeps to Mars, maybe?
But if some extraterrestrial object or mishap interposes?
If amnesia holds men and women hard
And makes them strangers to earth's glorious history?
These wild conjectures are not wild at all
They are feverish thoughts of a brain
That can't translate in words
The mountainous love it feels
For this dear abode,
And for all its fairy tales so far woven—
Oh earth, don't cease to be.
I don't desire for a better planet,
Neither dream for greater grandiloquent charm

In other possible arenas lone and far.
Let me not be permanent,
I'll shirk its mapped ruminations.
Just be there and be perennially wondrous
In the same way as you've always been.
I keep awake some night and pray
With the awakened silence over me:
I don't know of any supernovas or black-holes well
That, they say, cause deepest wonder for the laymen.
If I were an Apollo, I'd have surely
Carved out a boon from Zeus of permanence
For my dear, dear earth, my soul-mate.
In that case, I'd have sacrificed my obsession
For her, my dear beautiful earth.

28. The Orange Smile

Give me that orange smile
I want to preserve it
In my heart's innermost clove
How your cinnamon teeth white
And the eyes of embers twinkle
When you pour out the nectar
Of your perfect smile—O fair lady
You've transcended every obstacle
In your way to reach there
For obstacles are many, you'd agree
Your wan bun and poise in words
Show those past murky moments
When the good world deceived you
And made you disbelieve her innocuousness
But you kept faith in yourself
Like a high mountain you stood indifferent
To all challenges and won
The rouge of your inner beauty
Has touched the corners of your cheek
O, that the sunrays knew this smile
Your milky white skin hue
Is tinged with your heart's purity
It's lovely, it's otherworldly and fine

That has infected me hard
The trouble-torn humanity needs you,
O unknown! You can shed their burden
And make soul's struggles look puny
These hard times need you
And your precious transcendental smile

29. Toys of Time

We're the toys of time
Kept in the sun or slime
All our life we're made
To do what he commands
When life often demands
And heart too desires differing lore
We see time's closed door
"You're done", he says
And frontward he lays
Some vague choices open
And we not having enough sway
Over him, simply do obey
The forced up path in stock
And are apportioned some rock
Of a deed to be done
Life's past trodden ways
Seem like a dream that pays
Nothing but a sad remembrance
When we used to youthfully prance
In the warmth of the sunlight
That shone multi-hued and bright
And ignorantly obscured the cloak
Of futurity. How pigmy-sized humans soak

The drudgery of shattered vision
And humbly make a submission
To the need of the hour
For all so limited is our power.

30. Modern Abhimanyu

Even the moon shines in borrowed lights
After the dreariest, dismal stormy nights,
The little helpless ant girds up his loins
Each time he mutates in woe and joins
The normal nature's course
In deeds of the hour that endorse
The cyclic relevance of life's affair—
The skeletal stream after dry summer
Gathers rains in plenty and flows,
Throwing into oblivion its desiccated woes.
The heroic sun lies calm beyond the clouds
And piles might upon might to remove shrouds
Of bleak memory of dark overcast days,
And pierces the earth with his dazzling rays.
Never in your woe, however big it might seem,
Take pains for granted, and covertly deem
The overcast sun of your iron mind
To have been permanently confined
In chains utterly unbreakable, and lost
In mazy entanglements that Abhimanyu cost
His pain-bedraggled life in battle great,
And gave his life to all-determining fate.
You're no old citizen of an old clime

But a modern Abhimanyu with his sense of time.
Take the new tools varied and strong
That comprise parleys, thoughts and studies long,
We've technics, wit, whole lot of link
That the old Abhimanyu could hardly think.
Use them wise and test your might,
The jute-stalks only break when held tight.
A human's might and mien and morale
Is not so brittle that it'll derail,
Like the stalks so easily, my boy.
Stoke up the embers of your human soul
And upward fly with a clear-cut goal
That adversities may come, but they'll go
Like morning mist that flees the sunny show;
Be like a heart stout and tall
You'll find miracles that your way fall.

31. Nocturnal Revelry

It's past one at night
Drums and yells are heard
From a nearest household
Some worship is going on there
What worship? Some goddess, it looks
I can't sleep along with a multitude
That have sensitivity and slight niggle
To take them away
From the oblivion of sleep,
From the happy realm of sleep—
Indian Constitution lawfully gives
All sects to worship freely.
Maybe, this night's noisy reverence
Is an expression of that fundamental right.
It's a continuous process.
All through the year, the Bengalis—
I'm not cognizant of other Indians—
Start beating drums or broadcasting on microphones
The loud songs of their devotion to religion
And the Omnipotent One—
Can God dwell in such chaotic worship?
I'm not much sure truly.
All idea about God we have

Is that he symbolises perfection—
Perfection of physical and moral display.
God may symbolise idea only,
If not the anthropomorphic presence—
I must keep that for reservation.
Sometimes a mere idea performs miracles.
What are the worshippers' heads
Really crammed with, who
Render the still winter night
Raucous with repetitive barbarity?
The administration may know better
For they have also human ears.
It's a difficult time now:
Abnormalities galore every nook and corner
And are given social recognition.
Education hasn't done much
Where nonsense has prevailed.
In the history of the land
Independence we saw quarter
Of a century ago and yet
The shadows of dependency are larger—
It's the gene or the habit of the zone,
I don't decipher which one—
Certainly none is at leisure enough
To ruminate and act on it.
Things are running berserk each day
And culture engulfed by anti-culture

32. The Poem

Who writes a dreamy thing called poem?
Certainly a maniac who dreams big!
But what about a dream without a foothold
In the dreary hard ground of reality?
And what about this maniac
Without the knowledge of sanity?
A poem's a poem if it talks
Sense when nonsense looms large
Or holds a mirror up to the most ordinary;
That it designs to beautify,
For beauty is a formula and standard
That measures the scale of human success.
It's a judgemental yardstick forcing
Imaginary dialogues within the psyche
That remains ever active to participate
In the business of might-have-beens.
A poem not only speaks but ordains
For humanity a smooth way
When unevenness sprawls around;
A poem is the first light that illumined
The world in its first day of being
For, light only holds sway over darkness.
A poem is the torrential rain

Of summer that refreshes nature
And helps her get rid of all trash
A poem's a fairy's child born
Out of the womb of wonderment
A poem's the last anchor of a troubled race
That has ever bred complications
A poem's a happy outing in a field
Atop a hill that only offers endless marvels.
A poem's more than a religious preacher
For it never comes to deceive its believers.

33. Knowledge

Knowledge is pain.
The innocence of infancy
Is a blessing that covers
You from the dark secrets
Of life. The myriad woes
Of this world surface
As you go through chapters
Of human history besmeared
With mere brutal ignorance—
Density of your outward mirth
Gradually gets sliced up
With the knives of heartache
Seeping into you through conscience
And the humble humanity and pliancy
Of your inner core that throbs.
You get to realise the cruelty
Your fellow humans have suffered.
You ponder and wonder at the extent
The humans have reached in barbarity.
A human heart meant to be soft
Can't commit genocide,
Can't resort to beastly means
That have already been committed—

O remembrance thorny! How can I forgive

The perpetrators? Perhaps in no way ever.

There can't be a second Jesus—shouldn't be either.

For, barbarians never learn a lesson.

And when the books giving knowledge

Get crammed with their presence, it's time

We learn to discard chapters of barbaric history,

We need to make knowledge a pleasure, after all.

34. The North Wind

The north wind is rife today
I've resolved to face it
I'm facing it right in front
The cold breeze around the field
Gives me some unwelcome bidding
The dust and left away leaves
Have entangled my feet
The trees and the gray sky
Haven't yet risen from their wintry sleep
I have a query to the sky
'What are you for?'
All my life I've deemed you
As a sprawling presence, a formidable one
Now that I can smell the icy wind
And its multifarious lures
Recollected through my childhood filtration
This field, this green grass
The elephantine plantain leaves
That have gathered dust
This view of the sky filtered through the leaves
This recollection of old nostalgic scents
Ah, what a felicity in them
We can only helplessly feel this felicity

Seep through our inner being
But this mother feeling isn't all
When dark unfathomables shroud
The jovial mood of our outward nature
When the educated roam on the street
Like spectral and hopeless vagabonds
When the commoners' commonest
Greed for money decides the fate
Of the commoners themselves
Like a boomerang wound after elections
When the peasants revolt against
The autocratic government and starve
The innocent felicity gets mired
With cloudy uncertainty and dearth
The dearth of naturalness of humanity
Our natural gaiety gives in to practicality
Of a far primitivism, the animalish anomalies
That humanity often involves into it.
Life has this twofold affliction
I'm suddenly aware of an ocean
That since my consciousness was there
But hidden among the joys supreme
That life itself offered me
The receding anger of a hurtful mind
Is what matters the most, the everlasting
Pain of the civilized brains
O northern sky, do your best

To send forth more wintry days
Until the earth freezes for eternity
And you may live supreme for years.

• 63 •

35. No Room for Blunders

Even today, there is caste discrimination
Even today…
We have crossed two millennia
There are numerous films, books, laws
That propagate against all of it
Won't we learn?
Society still talks about Brahmins and low-caste people
Still 'dalits' are referred to as low and what not
Brahmins may get interrogated in big scams
And yet deserve reverence, for they are high-born
A dalit may excel in different high posts
And yet won't be sung about, for his ancestors
Used to serve in Brahmin families once…
Birth matters, not deeds, to the conservatives
Who don't know and abide by the essentials of modernity
How can an unscientific outlook, wrongly conceived as
religious,
Still decide the fate of some fresh lives, let alone
The thousands of life it has nipped in the bud
How can an individual be labelled as a low-born
By another human who has no control over birth
Do the discriminators deem themselves as God?

If there are books still that teach you about people
Deserving to be segregated thus, keep them aside
Or throw them into the mid-stream waters
They are conceived by devils' brains, devils
Who have misled society through subtle play of politics
B R Ambedkar knew it well
The boy who was bestially maltreated gave the society
Its first Constitution, which now decides the fate
Of a whole nation
The division of society on the basis of birth
Is the most primitive thought and act
That can exist in a twenty-first century nation
I have no grudge that I fulfil through these lines
Rather my mind is deeply pained
To see the extent to which thoughtless human psyche
May lead itself to—
The death or assassination of Luther King Jr
Who only dreamt the utopian equality of all people—
Whether one be black or white in the breast of America—
Still haunts just like the assassination of Abraham Lincoln
The black Africans and the low-caste Indians are soul-mates
In the same struggle for peace and happiness
Struggle without any real causes for it, although
The 'adivasis' (original residents) of India too face
Untold nightmarish calumnies for nothing
Things are rather made complicated by those
Whose mind-doors are eternally shut out

To the propriety of thought and feeling
The society we live in has many maladies
Let us stop discriminating, for it proves nonsensical
Let us admit our faults and move ahead
There are important things to do we must realise
We have to educate more people and spread
The sane lessons of philosophy and literature
We have to work speedily because thousands years
Of barbarity, and lack of true knowledge and love
For each other are to be redressed through dedication
We need more sacrifice, more than what the freedom fighters
Had smilingly done for us
We have to keep pace with the world
Science and technology are fast progressing
Let's make no more divisions and recognise our brothers
Who have been unduly and unwittingly wronged
History always follows us wherever we may be
Let's make a new history we may be proud of
In this age of globalisation we shouldn't lag behind anymore
There is no more room for blunders